Compliments of the author
and the remarkable team that made it happen

With much aloha,

SONGS
of the
Tradewinds

SONGS
of the
Tradewinds

RECOLLECTIONS OF HAWAIʻI

J. J. Meeker

PHOTOGRAPHY BY ***Galen Rowell***
FOREWORD BY ***Kris Kristofferson***

La Paz Press
PO Box 6126
Alameda, CA 94501

Distributed by Bess Press, www.besspress.com

Photo credits on page 180

Project Manager: Arnie Kotler Editing Services
Coproducer: Thea Chalmers
Hawaiian language advisors: Kahikāhealani Wight and Mike Atwood

Printed in China

Publishers Cataloguing-in-Publication Data

Names: Meeker, J. J., author. | Rowell, Galen A., photographer. | Kristofferson, Kris, writer of introduction.

Title: Songs of the tradewinds : recollections of Hawai‘i / J.J. Meeker ; photography by Galen Rowell ; foreword by Kris Kristofferson.

Other titles: Recollections of Hawai‘i

Description: Alameda, California : La Paz Press ; Honolulu : distributed by Bess Press, [2017]

Identifiers: ISBN: 978-0-692-67456-7

Subjects: LCSH: Hawaii—Poetry. | Hawaii—Pictorial works. | Hawaiians—Poetry. | Wilderness areas—Hawaii--Poetry. | Nature conservation—Hawaii—Poetry. | Fishing—Hawaii—Poetry. | Cultural awareness—Hawaii—Poetry. | American poetry—Hawaii.

Classification: LCC: PS3613.E373 S66 2017 | DDC: 811/.6--dc23

Contents

Rose Ranch, Ulupalakua, on the Slopes of Haleakala, Maui, 1865, oil painting by Enoch Wood Perry, Jr.

Foreword

We are children of the '50s, Meeker and I. Maybe the last generation to revel in the wonders of our natural environment without the awareness that we are rapidly destroying it. Witness the death of Idealism by assassination and war (Jim went to the breakfast for JFK in Fort Worth in the morning shortly before he flew to Dallas), replaced by a cynical cold-blooded materialism. We are perhaps uniquely equipped to appreciate the wonders of Creation. Born and raised in different parts of Texas (he in Fort Worth, I in Brownsville) we've been around the world together and back again. We ran in front of the bulls in Pamplona (summer of '60) and did other dangerous and exciting things since then—and wound up, incredibly, in the same small community on the green slopes of a volcano in the mid-Pacific.

Meeker's poems celebrate life in the passionate, joyful images of the island paradise in which he "dwells delighted"—the quivering and magic beauty of the fish, the wild, intoxicating fragrances of strange flowers. Always seeking

Order in Experience, the Poetic Eye finds meaning in the loving connection between the people and between the people and the earth. The truth is distilled into clear, tangible images, bursting with exuberance and the music of chants and ancient songs mixed with the music of the Heart and Blood.

Meeker's on the side of the angels, fighting to preserve this garden in which—like Helen Keller's *"Enchanted Wood"*—"The foliage is always green, where joy abides, where nightingales nest and sing, and where life and death are one in the presence of the Lord."

Luakaha (Morning), oil on canvas painting by Lionel Walden, c. 1916

Introduction

There is a part of Hawai'i, often called "The Heavenly Place" or "The Last Hawaiian Place," that is just that: a truly fortunate combination of volcano and rainforest, with rolling hills of green pasture and a charmed village set next to a clean blue sea, with rainbows after every shower.

Coupled with this beguiling landscape is a population of equally rare and harmonious characteristics. A mixture of races, a majority of the coast's present-day people are of part-Hawaiian descent, still sharing a daily life that is linked in time, through custom and tradition, back to the first Polynesian settlement of Maui.

It has always been this way. Evergreen and fertile, this stretch of volcanic slopes and valleys was highly prized by Kamehameha, the first king of all the Islands. His widow and regent, Queen Ka'ahumanu, was born by its picturesque bay, and King Kalākaua, the latter-day "Merrie Monarch," made his summer home here.

Following the sugar plantation's era of intensive agricultural production up until today, the land has remained seemingly unchanged. The fact that it is sparsely populated and undeveloped, for whatever reasons, is well-nigh miraculous, considering the frenzy of commercial growth the Islands have endured.

Of course, this place of enchantment and its way of life are threatened. Only because of its comparatively remote location could anyone consider intensive development of this treasure without national protest. There is no lack of housing and visitor accommodations with golf courses on the other side of the island, a few hours away by car. There is only a very small airport here and the residents want it to stay that way.

In spite of these facts and local resistance, serious change could come to this pastoral existence. A large part of the open land along several miles of road, coastline, and pasture and the only hotel and commercial property in the village are owned by entities sensitive to economic pressure. A whole community and its unique culture could be bought and sold and suffer much alteration and degradation in the process.

Hope and pray with native Hawaiians that our island Eden will pass into benign and permanent conservation, which will cherish and maintain this living heart of Hawai'i yet still gain by sharing its magnificent abundance.

With native prayers,
A dream you share
Is faith renewed,
Believe in liberty,
And destiny,
Believe with me,
From blue prairies
Of the Pacific,
Peace
And
Love to you,
Love indeed.

J. J. M.

A Hui Hou

Until We Meet Again

FOR BARBARA & GALEN ROWELL

The rainbow
Is a ring
Around the shadow
Of the plane
Upon the sea below.
The engines roar
And fling
A thousand images into being,
As we take flight
And our spirits
Take wing,
Through mansions of sun-dappled clouds,
Between
Mountains
Bowed low
Under sheets of rain,
Among towering-proud thunderheads,
Pouring waterfalls,

Sailing past white egrets
As they flock down,
Alighting
Onto horses'
Backs
With our starred hearts
Searching
For the tracks
Of other travelers
In the sky,
The miracle of Hawai'i,
Encircled
By
Aloha.

Nā Kani O Ke Aloha

The Sounds of Love

FOR DOROTHY AND BOB DEBOLT

Soaring into eternity,
Some will
Never
Be alone,
Enfolded into family,
Aloha ʻoe,
May you be loved,
These are
The treasured bones
Of kindness,
The framework of hope,
The scope
Of incomparable life
And laughter,
Forever after,
Down the river
Before the rain,
Riding the wind,

Season's change,
With native prayers
A dream you share is faith renewed,
Believe in liberty and destiny,
Believe with me,
From blue prairies
Of the Pacific,
Peace
And
Love to you,
Love indeed.

Dwell Delighted

Up
From dreaming,
In our deep sleep,
To the easy ceremonies
Of love
Between
Kānaka maoli,
Native Hawaiians,
And tantalizing girls,
Dealers in pearls beyond price,
Aloha nui loa,
Much love indeed,
I play
For my soul
With winning dice
And we meet,
Reverently,
Fervently,
Upon our bed
Of
Nā Lei,

Garlands of flowers,
With her
By my side,
Devil darkness
Never stays.

Holding Together

I send you praise
Out there above
And below,
In the water,
Benediction,
Submerged
Iridescent brilliance
In glittering streams,
All creation
Converging
Here,
Hurled up in
Radiant showers
Show me roads,
Show me goals
Of good intentions,
Pray for the rainbow
Pray for the rain
Again and again,
Below and above,
Go with our love:

Comfort children,
Comfort beasts,
Comfort pilgrims,
Eat my feast,
Sail my seas,
Swim with my fish,
God will not mock,
God grant
Your wish.

New Eden

Starfish in the surf,
Dolphins in the waves,
Can you see
My faintest blemish?
Will infinite mercy
Prevail at last?
Undiminished,
Sing in the streets
And the marketplace
But stay
In reach,
The fire in
Your chimney
Keeps me from
Grief—your love
Saves me from harm,
My friend and neighbor
Has steady heart and arm,
Come and share my dreams,
Please come and take my hand,

Come and bring harmony
To our promised land,
Reforest the height
And breadth
Of Eden,
Inhale
The air
Of Hawai'i
Leading—gentled,
The animals of new arks,
Feeding creation's seeds
Into an abundant earth,
From faraway depths,
The spirit wept
With joy,
At salvation's
Blessed birth.

Moonbows

Arousing intensity,
Stirred by her certainty,
Immersed in endearments,
Murmuring here;
Silken robes
Thrown upon my bed,
Smiling pillow
Beside my head,
Serenity,
Infinity's mother,
Effervescent springs,
Quintessence of wisdom,
With golden rings
In ears of jade,
Of fortunes told
And fortunes saved,
Sunrise
Shades
Of summer,
Hawaiian saints
Burn no bridges,
Burn the candles,

Pull the handle of Aloha's gate,
Ring the chimes of faith and trust,
Lovers always,
By compassion
Ever joined together.

The Rainbow Runner

Stunned,
Surprised,
Right before
My eyes,
Kindness transforms,
Nothing is harmed,
Paradise is laughing,
With angels massing
Into meteor showers,
Into wildflowers,
Molding hours into perfection,
Breaching whales touch sky,
Porpoises can fly,
Braving gravity's
Weight,
And we,
Embracing our faith,
Accepting our fate
Gratefully,

Joyfully,
Nui Ke Aloha,
Much love,
Fresh sprung
From the shores
Of these green islands.

The Eye of the Volcano

Explosion
On the rim,
In the center
Of the volcano,
Hawaiian goddess
Pele
Rising,
Pele
Dancing,
Between seething waves of the hardening lava flow,
The road still rain-soaked and smoking,
Baked hot by the sun,
Laughing,
Enchanting,
Slow,
Pele
Rising,
Pele
Dancing,
Nonchalant,
At her leisure,

Before the blast,
Before the blow,
Before the flames,
When the thunder
Of her jubilation
Shakes the earth for her pleasure,
Igniting even the mirth
Of
Ke Akua,
God,
Fabled sun
Descending through waving leaves,
Mere magic,
Pink and amber Shower trees.

Fisherman's Chapel

In fortune's
Farthest corners
Of the ocean,
Pulsing colors,
Resurgent peace
Lifting up with jumping mahimahi,
Queen of these shores,
Called up by fish-hunting wishes,
Good island witches with us,
Climbing new high horizons,
Holy eyes glimpsing forward into time;
Although you hear
God's horses
With bells on,
Until you see mahimahi leaping,
Until you smell her scent
Of the sea,
Until you hear the ring and feel the surge,
Hear the snap of the Sea King's trap,
A sound like the whistle of God,
Other ravings make no difference,

Other ravings make no sense,
The saving grace
Is in the raging race,
The inference divine,
Our ship's search
For mahimahi
A favorite church
Of mine.
(May God take care of fishermen.)

Ask Questions Later

When I am
Very old
And dark
And tanned
From the heat
Of the Pacific sun,
Hold the fans
Next to my heart and head,
And with sacred
Ancient groves
Of Umbrella trees
In place
Against the rain,
Just in case,
Harvest
Bliss
With Red Ginger
And night-blooming Jasmine,
And affection
With avid caresses,

Instead of inner-city sadness,
The madness of the sin
Of destructive pride,
By envy enslaved,
Forgotten
With her beloved presence,
Each day translated
Into the essence
Of our desire.

KOOL
Tide

Aloha Kamahaʻo
Wonderful Love

You move
With the music so sweetly
My spirit swells,
And with senses uplifted
I ascend
Into your spell,
Mahalo Nui Loa
Thank you very much
For such smiles,
Eyes brilliant with new allure
And old memories,
Mesmerizing Poincianas,
Scarlet Peacock-flower trees,
Softly—the calming breezes calling to me,
Scattering petals,
Spelling dusk,
Balm-scented nights,
Everything is right with us
And I lie down with ʻŌhiʻa blossom,
Her startling blooms and blood-red fervor

Turning sky-blue in our embrace,
My savage tamed,
Shifting winds
Cool our haven,
With elation,
Pleading my cause,
Unable to stay apart,
Spectacular hurtling star ablaze,
Fall here
And together,
As you remain in me,
I remain in you,
peace descending,
And love renewed.

Hawai'i Nei
This Beloved Hawai'i

Trusting souls,
Innocents in repose,
Trading soft blows,
Rubbing noses,
Swapping lies,
Swapping Lei,
Heartache flies,
Aloha stays,
Wine wits regarding breasts,
Playful jests,
Shuffling cards,
Laughing hard,
Winning darts of kindly wisdom,
Loving
Da kine,
The best,
Come
Put your heart
Where your mouth is
And belly up to some loving,

God knows in Hawaiʻi
Our kingdom is coming;
Showering—overpowering,
Tumultuous innuendo,
Irresistible—devouring,
Amorous crescendo,
Bounding fountains,
Vaulting towers,
Pumping volcano erupting flowers,
Racing past sadness into faith
And into belief again—safe,
Incandescent islands—shining,
All angels blessing
The cape of Hawaiʻi,
With rainbow lining.

Ka Lei Aloha
Beloved Child
For Danielle

Second sight and second life,
On the right track,
Joined with bright dolphins,
Racing horses hitting their stride,
In the wake of the fire of the Phoenix,
Snow on the mountain, snow on the moon,
Soon Hawaiian spirits casting spells,
Smile and nod at Danielle,
Ka Lei Aloha,
Beloved Child
And the lions of heaven,
Restoration on the shores of mist-filled mornings,
Coastal prisms bestowed by the sun and clear water,
Schisms filtered from the past into new agreement,
Heat near the surface,
Seven pools—seven priests,
Lightning never ceases,
The great wheel's ever-turning wonders,

My artful thief of love,
In possession of each heart
And I of hers,
Pure—sinless,
Parting tender petals,
Nature flung her cherubim
Into precious splendor,
Immutable fishermen of fate catch treasured souls,
Singing forever with reverend hosts,
Here together share—and toast them with light,
Thankful for rejoicing love
And truly priceless,
Peerless, delightful
Ka Lei Aloha.

Pinao
Dragonfly

The giants are out there,
We just have to find them,
The silhouette of the fishing rods with time suspended,
The lines extended—taut,
Geometry of endless horizons,
A hundred glowing mahimahi gliding in the mind,
Until the shrieking reel saves sinking hearts;
Part the waters of the monster channel
ʻAlenuihāhā,
Great billows smashing,
Between Hawaiʻi and East Maui's shores,
My hand fits into the palm of providence when fishing,
I sing my song to heaven,
Which casts traces of benevolence,
Like numberless sprays of dolphin upon our lives and
thrives upon our asking
And which sets me the task of masking my apes,
And reining in hot horses;
But what can you do about sharp double tongues?
Two against one in a fight,

The smack of careless pups biting in the back and in the hand,
Stalling union,
Happiness mangled and in ruins,
Held captive by hate,
Crisscrossed by hue and shade,
And still basking in the mid-day,
I am myself,
Not my possessions,
What you see is free for the asking,
Shimmering paths at our feet,
When the race is run, it is won,
When the story is told, it is done,
Our way guided by indigo tidal highways,
Tailwinds blow,
Pinao,
Dragonfly,
Show me home.

Hawaiian Girls

Ring around the moon,
The shy girl inside herself
Puts fragrant gardenias into her
Shining dark hair,
Reflections
On the wet palm leaves,
Safe from thieves
And haunted faces,
Pulses beating faster,
Quickly fleeing shadows,
Languorous hibiscus in the dusky light,
Sundown streaking,
The hot breath of the mango dragon,
From out of celestial smoke
Come translucent pearls,
Intriguing
Ever fresh,
Hawaiian girls,
Under my lure,

Bewitching—quick
Sudden swirls,
Hawaiian girls,
Quivering senses,
Past defenses,
Waves unfurl,
Let me leap the fences,
Hawaiian girls,
Hawaiian girls.

Ānuenue
Rainbow

You fell out
Of the mists
Into
The middle of my road,
Quickening muse,
Take up my load,
Send the lamb
From out of your fold,
Save our children
Before they grow old,
Tell me stories
That never
Have been told,
You are an evanescent smoke ring
In firelight,
Come to me enkindled
By burning primal dreams,

With the fisherman's daughter blessing me,
Pearlescent silver fins
And fertile crescent,
My golden fish,
My mahimahi.

Hawaiian Soldiers

With Hawaiian soldiers
Day and night,
Courage beckons,
No fear—no fright,
Moved by honor and innocence,
Healing Aloha is flung from heaven
Into my soul
And never parting,
Keeps all anxiety away
And we march free
With Hawaiian soldiers;
Burnished stars,
Hawaiian knights,
Guitars beseeching fights
With dragonflies,
Daring darkness,
Sparkling sights,
Please send us space ships,
God is not cheap!
Chanting
Nā Wāhine—

Women
With beautiful big hips,
Hawaiian chiefs,
Feel the music,
Dance my dance
Dance the hula,
You can't reach higher,
Heart's desire,
Take your chances
With Hawaiian soldiers.

Island Rains

Daring thoughts
Pulsing—clots
Restless flesh,
Fingers mesh,
Enlarging veins,
Island rains.
Moonrise brightens,
Our mouths tighten,
Bodies tense,
Fever jells,
Senses meld,
Island rains.
Hair glistens,
Smell—listen,
Urgent—compelling,
Nature swelling,
Bursting forth,
Island rains.
Rushing—worth
Spilling treasure
Without measure,
Giving comfort

Without pressure,
Island rains.
Racing blood,
Racing mood,
Racing moon,
Racing doom,
Whispering beauty,
Island rains.
Ocean into infinity,
With valley waterfall's
Exalted sublimity,
Her morning glories
Mounting—soaring,
Island rains.
Light through clouds,
Piercing—pouring,
Ends the reign
Of care and distress,
Imparadised here together,
Island rains.

Mana
Spiritual Power

The arch
Of the rainbow,
Prismatic bull's-eye,
The arc of change throws its image
Onto the other side of the shade,
Etched by flame,
Playing as if life were the sacred game indeed,
Better to hear the click of Divinity's teeth than feel them,
What you need is salt from the sea
And my arms
And my lips,
Always young,
Hearts strung side by side,
Hung together
Never will die;
Can you make too much
Of the rainbow?
Can you try too hard
For the truth?
Has God grown weary

Of earth's game show?
Does childhood show the mark
Of fear's tooth?
Give us the best of the ocean,
Again,
Blessings from above and below,
Rise up with ascending emotion,
Fly high
For our spirits to know,
The tender green of eternal spring,
Like fragrance
Compelling,
The taste of heaven,
Here with us,
Enchantment,
Dwelling.

Mahalo Ke Akua
Thank You, God

In all,
I must
Have seen
A hundred whales or more
This past year,
I saw
A pod today
Of six big ones
And two young calves,
Glistening in the sun,
Within the waves,
Near the coast,
Spouting fountains of the ocean,
As they turn upon their sides,
Flecks of rainbows
In their wake
And

I could see great eyes
That seem big
As pie plates
And hear
The sounds,
As loud as rifle shots,
Of their gigantic fins
Pounding upon the water,
Demi-godlings of this world,
Strings of swarthy pearls
Strung between the islands,
Descending through blue depths
As in dreams,
The luminous designs
Of
Mystery.

Rainbirds

In Hawai'i,
Ahi is the name of fire
And also a fish;
Our desire for decent lives,
Volcano prodding truth from idle wishing,
Proof of regeneration climbing with the blessed turtle
Awakened from its consecrated sleep,
Moving up onto the edge of the beard of Maui,
Alpha tango,
Island geckos and ripened mangos,
Mother marlin thrust my lure in deep,
Rename heaven, it is still as sweet,
Have I become so jaded no help is needed to save my soul,
As the swaggering world grows old and dirty?
Time to stand up once more for youth;
Seen through clouded pitchers of margaritas,
Crowded—exhausted victims,
Pictures of life as seen from the visions
Of well-meaning sinners,
Between the day and night,
Thrones of equality begin to form and dim old dawns,

Flocks of native geese
And cats from kindred litters of the sun,
Won by sacred lips and angelic face,
Hints from God,
Shod with halos of rainbows,
A soft voice calling,
The songbird charmed,
Endearing,
Enduring,
Alpha tango,
Island geckos and ripened mangos,
Beginning and the end,
Send laughter to the stars,
Safe, content,
Blessed
In our Hawai‘i.

Refrains of Angels

A great branch falling,
A tree is down,
Night birds calling across the valley
Sound the spell of evening glow,
When
Below,
Winds uncover moonrise
In the strongholds of the rainforest;
Rest
Without
Grown-up children of war
Quarreling into horror,
Sounds of shadows
With no tomorrows,
Weep without me,
This is where
We sleep,
In any case,
Without misgiving,
The favor of fulfillment and access to deity
Keep in vision,

The fission of faith's conviction
Overriding all confusion
About the world's illusions;
In the bowers of our retreats,
Showers cease,
Love in cadence
With the heartbeat
Of my islands,
Warmth in place of the cold,
God's laughter,
Better than gold.

Aloha Pumehana
Warmhearted Love

Casting nets of affection,
Working high above
The crowd,
Catch the clown if he falls,
Call out loud
For justice always,
My place
Right here by her side,
Pity brushed the tears
From anger's eyes,
Aroused,
Despair must die
One more time
With the birth of Aloha,
Old and ageless friends,
Ardent pleas
Of the spirit,
Torn from what stars?

Aquamarine
Schemes of persistence,
Crashing water meets rock,
The shock of resistance,
Sympathy pushing through
The veils of antipathy,
Singing,
Over the wall,
Enthralled by sweet naivete,
Home at last,
At the last
Not least,
Saved again
By the sea
Of peace.

The Layman's Liturgy

Curl around
My body,
Blazing Bougainvillea vine,
And grow into a tree,
Surrounding us
And we will raise ourselves
Up to refuge;
Oh—my Marie,
Let the waves wash over you
And me,
Our tribe of love,
Each one a chief,
He and
She
And we two together
Locked into this reality,
Bounteous,
Our God
The God of mercy,
All lovers led like us,
Laid down and placed

By cunning love
into bed,
Inspiring vibrant dreams,
Entwined in sensuality and expectation,
With her,
Indulgent mate
In carnival mood,
My true friend in flesh
And deed,
Superb,
Euphoric
Electricity.

Haleakalā
House of the Sun
FOR TRUDY TAYLOR

Startled,
The dove
Flew out
From her rest
Toward the evening sky,
My songs fly
By her side,
Star seeds
Need
The comfort and confidence
Of love,
The marvelous light of dawns'
Shot of gold,
And sensational
Hot-red sundowns,
In recollection
Never dim
Or ever dying,

Brightening
Lanterns for the soul,
The constancy
Of spring,
To be free
And at ease
Upon the splendid wings
Of hope.

Aloha ʻĀina
Love for the Land

A grove of Koa trees,
A Centuri
And Arcturus,
My islands and my archers,
All together,
Not about to want out
Of our earthly heaven
Undaunted Hawaiians
Flaunt their
Mana,
Spiritual power,
Looming from the past,
Rivers of music,
And regal dancing,
The incarnation of sacred forces;
Wandering,
Once far from grace,
Stand now
With
Aloha ʻāina,

Love for the land,
Rely on the navigator,
Holy—beaming,
The light within humanity,
Shows me liberty,
And beauty
Rocks—not sand,
Dreamers and pure loving,
Revealing prophecies of peace,
Maui's sure feasts,
Magnificent,
Unplanned.

Hana Hou
One More Time

You know I would like to stay
And help you with the masses,
But late at night pictures crash into my head,
Views of cities and too many people living lies,
Sand and shadow sharks swimming through the dark
To households they despise,
Whining,
Dining on death,
Taking advantage of bars to be their reward
And to lead their paths to bed,
Shining noonday sun cast me new fortunes,
Must I roll dice over and forever,
A feather in another's cap?
Island girl and leviathan angels,
Maps of anguished eyes
Combined with muffled cries,
Drained of feeling,
Back in the blues,
Praying you choose me,
Incendiary and easy lover,

Rival to the risen moon;
Love blown to bits,
To be rung back by trumpets,
Strummed by lightning,
Stunned by tightening bolts of affection,
In new directions
Local colts start the procession,
Bucking, right through the roof,
Roaming,
Romantic,
All bold heroes,
Walk like giants,
Bathed in streams of glory,
Hawaiian story talk
Told forever.

Two Hula Trances

Weave perfumed
Pīkake
Jasmine flowers
Into your hair,
In rainforest farms
Come into my heart
And let me love you
Once again and forever,
As we exult in jungle halls,
Captivated
By a gentle call
To surrender
To her arms
Of perfect
Celebration;

With no pretense,
Kids remain what they are
In Hawaiʻi,
They never learn

To doubt the dreams which carry them,
Tall—speechless,
Drifting afar in their minds,
Visions of places and things
Not as they exist
But as they should be and will,
God willing,
When
Voices of desperate children in need
Are heard
And fill the world
With righteous pleas
And mercy's healing peace.

Fishing Forever

Flinging
Language like
Flaming arrows in old western movies
Hawaiians throw the gauntlet down,
Here in the West,
Hoa Aloha,
Friend,
Do your best
Or be the clown,
While the rest of mankind festers,
Spiritual kettles
Barely
Steaming
On back burners,
The Hawaiians still take life with play
Seriously,
Paniolo
Pacific cowboys
Of the open ocean,
Poised for joyful roundup
Where re-creation rises

With the sun
Each day,
Invoke the living God
Of fishermen,
Pray we will be taken up,
And drain the lucky cup
When mahimahi sups again with us,
(Open sesame),
Betting on fishing
In sweet eternity.
(You can't eat money.)

Pono

Righteousness

FOR FR. FRANCIS SHIMONO AND MSGR. LEO LUCERO

I never would have been
A morning prayer man
Particularly,
But with them,
In my mind
Denying the evil eye,
Trembling wings of dragonflies
Proclaimed each day a holiday
With the smell of fresh hay
In the opulent fields of summer.
Laughing to myself,
Not quite to blame,
Aloha's net of memories catch me all the same
And we laugh together,
Tethering the horses of childhood
In pastures by sacred pools;
Deity may choose to be
On these hills and in these streams,

Beneficent—bemused,
Receiving each day,
Lapping and loving
In the waves of children,
Libations and ablutions,
Absolution in the blessings of the water;
With redoubled paternity,
We rejoice in perpetuity in fraternity with the sea,
Fishing for love forever,
Catching
The wishes
Of
God.

Hibiscus

Big island
Triumphant,
With seeming never
Ceasing sunsets,
Exquisite
Seaside hibiscus,
Seizes my attention—yet
The distant mountain
Ignites with heat
And moves
Into my reverie,
Integrity
Stalking truth,
Loving friendship rejecting
Indifference,
Endearing,
Caressing
Hawaiian flowers,
Goodnight darlings,
Coming for us,
Caring for us,

Lovely starlings
Stabbing shadows,
Tearing dimming twilight
All asunder,
Granting for us
Midnight's
Thunder,
Granting for us
Heaven's
Wonder.

The Smile of the Dove

Flamboyant,
Clairvoyant,
Praying to be on the side of compassion,
Circling cranes,
Abounding grace,
Are we two
Mated,
Matching horses?
Rampaging,
Racing,
Since the day we met?
Is it catch or am I caught?
Am I the net or am I the butterfly?
In pastoral island settings,
Scenes as conceived by Gauguin;
Enticed,
Entrapped,
Shy manta ray swaying,
She traded
Me in
For her bottles,

Empty in the end,
Until her price was met,
By loving her so much,
Fragile to the touch,
Constant brushes with the past,
And love until the last,
Her waving hands
An easy memory.

Pacifica

Palaces of stars above,
Over here
Where it's never all dark,
And cherished friends
Are children of sailors
And the tradewinds,
Ke Aloha o Hawai'i,
The love of Hawai'i,
When these daughters of Eve
Meet the sons of Maui
With time and space
Enough
For blissful reconciliation,
When all are saved
From a second fall,
Full sails in the evening,
Smiling mother moon
And
Bright shining
Manalo,
Venus,

Dreaming of their islands,
Standing in clouds of orchids
And
Pausing—
For liberty
Knows my kiss
And love
Cannot
Miss.

Holy Marlin

Love's pure gift,
The sea's free spirit,
Light lifts hope
From darkened shoals
Onto my line
And changing oceans,
Changing times,
Life slow-motions
Into heaven,
Beyond all rhyme
And into reason,
The perfection tense,
Slick as the line,
Quick as the hook,
Water like wine,
Let divinity
Look behind—for them
And ahead
For me
And Holy Marlin.

Memos from the Past

Either
The world
Made right,
The sight
Of paradise
Reclaimed
Or
This place
By the sea
Could never
Be the same
If the waters
Come
Up this far,
Shattering,
Huge
Tsunamis,
Tidal waves,
Of terror
From out
Of the dark

That can pull apart
The coast,
Aloha ʻāina,
Love for the land,
Sad dog
Eat dog
And abandon all
Hope,
For houses
Built
Upon sand.

Angel Daughters

Speaking of affection
And desire,
In the half-light,
By the campsite,
Fate still controls the volcano,
So for the time being is what we possess,
Since all of our tomorrows
Are in the eyes of faith and hope only
Until we are taken into stars,
Lightning flashes from the sea,
Do not slip on
Self
Sufficiency,
Angelic guardians
Still look after us,
Thunder across the water,
The cleansing rain now soon begins,
And sin dies
A natural death,
Retreating into the dark,
When with the sun

We then are raised and saved
From scheming hands and hardened hearts
As angel daughters start the dance
And forever in eternity
Is rapturous
After all,
It is always
Today
In the hallways
Of the Lord.

Life of the World

She wants the earth,
I want the sky,
Hurled from her heart into mine,
To be forgiving is Aloha
Indeed,
I saw visions
Descending
From a flashing,
Flowing Shower tree,
Planting sparkling revelation,
Introducing destiny in western oceans and easy fishing boats;
New ascending volcanoes thrusting crimson wings of lava
Always
Seaward,
Coming into view,
Racing past black holes,
Freeing blasted souls,
The art of adventure,
Rebirth for the old,
From the sea—plunging whales,
And mahimahi pulsing colors,

Island voices calling,
Insisting upon our love,
Time upon time again,
Doubt not
That now is always when it counts,
Your lover lets you win,
There is a God
And between you and God
The laughter
Never
Ends.

All Things New

Neighboring trees,
Their branches intermingled,
The succulent kissing of blossoms
Clustered,
Pink and white,
In cool alcoves,
The pungent caress
Of perfumed
Nā Lei,
Garlands of flowers,
Upon our lover's shoulders,
Express your needs as gaudy orchids display
Pale magenta charms with coral seeds trailing,
Engaging island families,
Interpret love from old scriptures
Win my wine,
Eat with me the loaves of joyous leavening,
In the evening,
Faith's reveille sounds again,
Elijah and Confucius,

Mahatma Gandhi
And
Smiling Buddha,
Chant with dancing faun
And Christ and the Mother
In Paradise
Together,
Perfect,
Melodious,
With flowered crowns
Upon immortal brows,
Akua, Adonai, the Trinity,
Always divinity
In the heart
Of Hawaiʻi.

Other Sightings of Simple Grace

A pealing of bells,
Singing saints,
With wondrous maidens,
Can you see
My windward forests,
Rainbow-laden,
Shade from the heat,
Over here
Behind
The opening gates,
Opening
For you
And me,
With
Buds of mercy,
Growing beneath
Sun-swept mountains
Among the mango groves,
Orange and yellow
Bird of Paradise,
Cascading waterfalls,

Playing gourd-drums and guitars,
Be-flowered island armies trod
The wine press
Of each day,
Delighting
In other sightings
Of simple
Grace.

Perpetual Light

Where
The shores
Of paradisiacal beaches
Meet the sea,
Sanctuary
For me,
The favor
Of facing my beliefs,
And believing
In my faith,
Rejoicing alone
And in the company
Of native priests,
Dreams summoned
Again by memories,
Songs streaming,
Remembrances of the Mother,
Caught by prayer
Before the sun
Goes down
Along the slope

Of the volcano,
Our high frontier,
The moon makes
Her stunning resurrection
To the east,
The boundless delights
Of Deity,
Our trees
Of life
Have innocence and order
For their roots
And here all
Are offshoots
Of angels.

A Truck Full of Lei
Flower Wreaths

Rain bringer,
Drought breaker,
Remember
Free will
Gives us
The mode
Of choosing
Our approach,
To each
Our own nirvana,
The spirit's hosannas
From heaven
In Splendid
Innocence,
Native island dancers,
With Jade Vine Lei
Of opalescent colors,
Towers of light,
No longer bathed

By shadows,
Our faith
Grows apace,
With laughter and Aloha,
Blessed always
Is this
Place.

Paradise Is a Walled Garden

Both sacred
And
Profane,
Love regains
Her hold
On me,
Legend revealed
In seas of color,
Multi-hued
Plumeria trees,
Scented ecstasies
Unexpected
In luxuriant branches blooming
On a summer afternoon,
And no one there
But you and me,
Both carnal
And divine,
God is love
And love is our God,
And love

Is our drug
From now on,
Like the oldest,
Rarest of wines,
Undenied adoration
Today
At last,
With you in Paradise.

Nui Ke Aloha
Love Indeed

In new millenniums,
From old dominions,
When light meets dark,
Growth begins,
Fingers of promise through sleeves of sin,
I know that my body is not as big as my ego,
Ergo,
I think—therefore,
I am a lamb
Waiting to be a sheep,
A ram,
A man,
At ease,
With the Queen of Hearts
And all aces in my hand,
Great grand vistas,
A reservoir of contentment
Found with friends,
Roaming in old forests,
Tradewinds in chorus,

Circling salty saints,
Painted by the rainbow into walled gardens,
The eye of the turtle upon us,
Mynah birds strutting,
Let the lady have her way,
After all this time,
Her desire will lead us safely
Through mighty waters,
Stirring,
Rampant flags
Breach new winds,
Bring me consummation,
Once again,
God is that God is,
Always,
I believe I am Hers,
I pray I am His.

Island Lights

Coursing up like comets
Through veins of hope,
Hot into the heart of the Pacific,
Denying darkness,
Some like minstrels,
Some like priests,
The dawning of the people's chiefs,
The doom of tinsel trumpets,
The music of the spheres
Channeled into blues,
Rising through space,
Divine providence
Plots our cause and behind the constellations pausing,
Sends beams of enlightenment soaring into tomorrow,
Enlarged again by holy bravado,
Reason enough to hold on fast
When vanity vies with avarice,
Bloodied but once and unbowed now,
Our God reckons and our fate beckons,
Don't doubt the precious second chances
That love can give us here in these splendid lands,

Peace dependent upon hands of friendship,
Our good fortune to be alive,
A reminder to honor one another,
Friends and lovers
And form a circle of the sun's promise,
A sacred equation's sum:
When all are as one,
Expectations done,
The Island kingdoms
Come.

Equanimity

No matter what
I had planned,
How was I to know
Our bodies sing,
Beneath our hands,
Passing understanding
In common fashion?
Head upon heartbeat,
With kisses
Encompassing realities
Beyond dreams,
With time to breathe,
Here we are part of the place,
Here we can proceed with dignity and ease
As infinity recedes into laughter flashes,
Storming after thunderclouds
With midnight dashes for the sun,
Na Lei Aloha,
Garlands of love
Halos of rainbows and lightning,
Fixed forever

Around divinity's neck and hair,
Take care for your lovers,
Discover bountiful truth,
All our aspirations
Are fulfilled in tranquility,
With belief
In
Love's
Sweet remedies.

Vessels of Mercy

Holding on
To love,
Just as if
They
Are calling you
From
The ocean
Out there,
The blue surf
Curled up
In Divinity's fingers,
Drums from the deep,
Sounding,
Mighty Humpback whales,
Flashing out
Of the sea,
Dancing on the waves
And diving again,
Erupting
With
Giant white sprays

Of splashing foam,
Aloha,
Go out
To play
With God
And you never
Play
Alone.

ABOUT THE AUTHOR

J. J. Meeker: A Connecting Force

In the creation of all things beautiful, there is a connecting force—a glue that binds, a thread that ties, a spine that centers, a bridge that spans. James J. Meeker has, in his unique way, been that force of nature, linking and supporting some of the most creative minds of the 20th and 21st centuries. He achieved this with no aim for personal gain, but simply as opportunities arose. He is that rare breed of man whose instinct is always to extend both his hands and be a friend.

Jim was born on a farm near Fort Worth, Texas, called Indian Springs. It was a time of quiet innocence in a land of extraordinary beauty, and Jim spent countless hours wandering the pasturelands barefoot, scrambling up massive oak trees, and devouring every book he could find. He often brought his reading with him onto the wildest parts of the farm, traversing thorny vines by laying his books upon the stickers and stepping carefully from book to book. Literally, books were his

Jim Meeker standing in front of Standard Station, Amarillo, Texas, *1963, Ed Ruscha. Oil on canvas. 64½ x 121¾ in. Hood Museum of Art, Dartmouth College, Hanover, New Hampshire; gift of James Meeker, Class of 1958, in memory of Lee English, Class of 1958, scholar, poet, athlete and friend to all. © Ed Ruscha.*

pathway. Jim grew up deeply connected to the natural world, reflected in the places he's chosen to live and the poetry and prose he's written.

Meeker's passionate curiosity has also propelled him toward mischief and wonder. After pursuing both throughout the world in his twenties, his family's needs drew him back to Texas. While there, he was the art columnist for the *Fort Worth Star-Telegram* (with the largest Sunday circulation in Texas), worked at the Kimbell Art Museum and the Amon Carter Museum of American Art, was very active in starting an independent school, Fort Worth Country Day, and served on the board of the Modern Art Museum of Fort Worth—all endeavors which helped him know many of the great contemporary musicians, artists, and architects of his time.

When friends of friends of the art world—from the US and abroad—found themselves in Texas, they were encouraged to look up Jim Meeker, and unintentionally he developed a reputation for hosting gatherings at his art-friendly, music-loving home. Smart, charming Texas locals mixed with provocative visitors who, more often than not, represented an exciting chapter of American and European counterculture. Speaking to Jim's granddaughter Danielle Lei Aloha Atwood, Mickey Raphael, who has played harmonica alongside Willie Nelson since the 1970s, described Jim as a man who provides artists and musicians with "spiritual encouragement."

Jim Meeker's love of people, art, and music has led to hundreds of friendships, a compliment he hears frequently even today. Jim always had a good sense about art, and his homes have been filled with vibrant, forward-thinking paintings. Journalist Margo Roosevelt, whose son is Jim's godson, says, "J.J. was so far ahead of his time that many people are still catching up." When artists would call and say, "I've got to get five hundred bucks for rent by next month," Jim would ask, "Can you take two payments?" It is his nature to offer whatever he has, and in return he'd receive these treasures. Jim knew Andy Warhol, for example, and acquired a set of ten Marilyn Monroe lithographs for $50 each. Later, along with four friends, he commissioned Warhol to make five oil-on-canvas portraits of Dennis Hopper in his *Easy Rider* outfit. Dennis was Jim's longtime friend, and he stayed at his home whenever he was in Taos. Ken Price and Ed Ruscha, two California artists Jim met in those days, are among the world's most celebrated artists. They remain close, and Jim has collected and donated their works to museums and schools—notably, to commemorate fellow Texan classmate Lee English's untimely death. Jim gave what is now an internationally celebrated Ruscha painting, *Standard Station, Amarillo, Texas*, to his alma mater, Dartmouth.

Alongside the tremendous friendships that have defined much of Jim's path has been a lifelong spiritual quest. After a near plane crash at night in the middle of the Atlantic, Jim promised God he would do something for Him, and through that promise met Father Leo Lucero in Santa Fe, New Mexico, provided the last-minute, necessary resources to renovate the sanctuary of the Guadalupe Virgin, the oldest monument to her in the US, and eventually converted to Catholicism himself. Later, while recovering from a car accident, Jim met Bob and Dorothy DeBolt, founders of Adopt A Special Kid. The DeBolts point out that his support has been pivotal to AASK's success, and he has devoted himself to helping place thousands of kids, many considered unadoptable, into permanent homes without charging a fee. This blessing was made possible thanks to the perseverance of "the incomparable" Nancy Hamon, AASK's largest donor and Jim's dear friend.

In 1980 Jim, his godson Paul, and a group of his friends traveled to Hawai'i, and Jim immediately fell in love with the land and the people. Soon after, he persuaded his girlfriend to return with him. They checked in at the Hotel Hāna-Maui and ended up staying for a year and a half. Jim then bought a house in Hāna and was based there for more than

twenty years. Father Francis Shimono, Hāna's Catholic priest in those years, described Jim as "a permanent, local, traveling resident." Jim feels that God is with him when he is in Hawai'i—in the fragrant air, the sunrises and sunsets, the people and the Aloha. The search for meaning that has driven Jim his whole life feels satisfied when he's there.

On one occasion when Jim needed to spend more time on the mainland but felt reluctant to leave, he confided in a local elder. "I hate to leave Hāna," he said. "I'm afraid I'll forget about it, and people will forget me." The man looked at him, smiled deeply, and replied, "Jim, everybody here knows you have Aloha for Hāna in your heart. You won't forget us, and we won't forget you." Jim's love for Hawai'i continues, and whenever he's there, he's treated as an honored and trusted friend.

In the 1980s, Bill Getty introduced Jim to Barbara and Galen Rowell in San Francisco. By then, Galen was recognized as one of the world's great outdoor photographers. He'd climbed the world's tallest peaks and taken spectacular photos of them. Jim, with his keen eye for art, deeply admired Galen's work and enjoyed being with Galen and Barbara—going to dinner and sharing time in Galen's Berkeley studio.

In 1993, Galen showed Jim *Caribbean Sea, the specter of the Brocken*, a photo he'd taken of a beautiful circular rainbow that had formed around the shadow of their small plane, piloted by Barbara, on the water below. Jim had just written a poem about exactly that image, and Galen offered him the photo. Then he said, "Have a look at these photos I took in Hawai'i." Jim was stunned by their extraordinary beauty, and immediately acquired nonexclusive rights to reproduce them in the book about Hawai'i he'd always dreamed of, which you now hold in your hands.

Words and poems come to Jim spontaneously, and he writes them down on whatever paper he can find, later pulling them together and polishing them. He is a natural lyricist, and his boundless affection, gratitude, and compassion are the bass line throughout his poems, or songs as he prefers to call them. Meeker's words reflect his journeyed, evolved relationship with God, the little boy who found comfort and wonder scrambling up ancient oak trees in Texas, and his deep Aloha for the life and spirit of Hawai'i. A cherished friend of Jim's, the late and very great guitarist Stephen Bruton, left a voicemail for him shortly before Stephen passed on:

"It's about time you took a bow for all you've done for everybody else. You know, in all honesty, I've never seen anybody stand in the wings and basically connect everybody I know. You are the catalyst, and I love ya', and you've done

Stephen Bruton © Jim Marshall Photography LLC.

nothing but great things for me and I'll be there for you, anytime, and every time."

Jim is not one for taking bows, despite the fact that he has done nothing but great things for myriad people ranging from high celebrities to highway hippies. In his modest way, he continues to be a catalyst and connecting force, offering his beaming smile, stories of times wild and divine, and outstretched hands to everyone he meets.

Galen and Barbara Rowell © Frans Lanting/Corbis.

Author and photographer biographies by Domenica Alioto

ABOUT THE PHOTOGRAPHER

Galen Rowell:

Photos as Timeless & Powerful as Nature Itself

Galen Avery Rowell was a world-renowned nature photographer and global explorer. His insatiable curiosity, taste for adventure, and understanding of light translated into a livelihood that took him to both poles and on more than fifty expeditions through the wildest mountain regions on the planet. He was considered a true pioneer of photojournalism, and for that received numerous honors, including the prestigious Ansel Adams Award for his contributions to the art of wilderness photography and the Lowell Thomas Award for Travel Photography. In addition, he was named Yosemite's Photographer Laureate and the Time/CNN Hero of the Planet. His gentle observations accompanied his vivid work in eighteen books, including the acclaimed *Mountain Light: In Search of the Dynamic Landscape.* Galen's stunning photographs gave him an internationally respected reputation for capturing and delivering the natural world. As Tom Brokaw recognized, "Galen Rowell … shared his vision with—click—the release of a shutter, creating photographs as timeless, as stunning, and as powerful as nature itself."

Galen met **Barbara Cushman Rowell** in April 1981, while she was working for The North Face as the director of PR. Born in Hawai'i and raised in Texas and California, she hired Galen to write text about a parka and a backpack for her company's catalog. They fell in love within the week and were married several months later. The following year, Barbara quit her job and joined Galen and Robert Redford on a monthlong trek in Nepal. After they returned home, she directed her energy toward promoting Galen's work before striking out in search of her own passion for flying and travel in Central and South America. An accomplished pilot, Barbara authored *Patagonia: Flying South: A Pilot's Inner Journey*, outlining her navigation of a 25,000-mile adventure through Latin America and sharing how it allowed her to discover unrealized self-confidence and vast reserves of strength.

Together, the intrepid pair established Mountain Light, a multifaceted business and gallery that housed hundreds of their photographs. After decades of voyages and exploration, Galen and Barbara moved their home and the Mountain

Light operations to Bishop, California, in the stunning Eastern Sierra they loved so dearly, where their work is still on display.

In August 2002, Galen and Barbara Rowell were killed in a plane crash near Bishop. Jim dedicates this book to his dear friends Galen and Barbara, in memory of their gentle kindness, zeal for life, unending courage, and the lightness they brought to every day.

To Jim,
kindred spirit of so many
things we both care about —
Your friend, Galen Rowell

Photographs

All photographs © by Galen Rowell/Mountain Light unless otherwise noted

p. 2 360° Rainbow over Na Pali Coast / with Galen's hand, Kauaʻi, 1993.

p. 7 Wailea Coast, Maui, 1993.

p. 12 Hula Girls, by Bob Wade.

p. 16 Caribbean Sea, the specter of the Brocken, 1991.

p. 20 Lava pouring into the sea, Hawaiʻi Volcanoes National Park, 1993.

p. 26 Road to top of Haleakalā Crater (10,023 ft.), Maui, 1993.

p. 30 Sugarcane fields, North Coast Hawaiʻi Island, 1993.

p. 34 Kilohana Crater, Kauaʻi, 1993.

p. 37 Blowhole near Poʻipu, Kauaʻi, 1993.

p. 40 Sugarcane fields, Maui, 1993.

p. 44 Lava in Puʻu Oʻo Crater, Hawaiʻi Volcanoes National Park, 1993.

p. 48 Suzy Eastman's flower farm, Kapaʻa Kauaʻi, 1993.

p. 51 Traditional store, Paʻia, Maui, 1993.

p. 54 Waterfalls near Waipiʻo, North Coast, Hawaiʻi Island, 1993.

p. 58 ʻŌhiʻa tree over lava, Hawaiʻi Volcanoes National Park, 1993.

p. 61 Silversword (ʻāhinahina), Haleakalā Crater, 1985, by Thea Chalmers.

p. 64 Jacaranda tree beside road to Haleakalā, Maui, 1993.

p. 67 Molokini Island off of Maui, 1993.

p. 70 Rainbow over wild Na Pali Coast, Kauaʻi, 1993.

p. 76 Mauna Kea (13,796 ft.) from the Kona Coast, Hawaiʻi Island, 1993.

p. 82 Nēnē, Hawaiian goose (state bird), Haleakalā Crater, 1985, by Thea Chalmers.

p. 88 Hawai'i Volcanoes National Park, Hawai'i Island, 1993.

p. 91 Kāne'ohe Bay, North Shore, O'ahu, 1993.

p. 94 Lahaina, Maui, 1993.

p. 98 Haleakalā Crater, Haleakalā National Park, Maui, 1993.

p. 102 Highlands at the top of West Maui forest reserve, Maui, 1993.

p. 106 Wailea Coast, Maui, 1993.

p. 109 Maui beach, 1993.

p. 112 Lahaina, Maui, 1993.

p. 118 Wildflowers erupt in Waimea Canyon after Hurricane Iniki, Kaua'i, 1992.

p. 124 Southwest Coast of Moloka'i, 1993.

p. 128 Lahaina, Maui, 1993.

p. 132 Haleakalā Crater, Haleakalā National Park, Maui, 1993.

p. 136 Lava pouring into the sea, Hawai'i Volcanoes National Park, 1993.

p. 140 Rainbow over wild Na Pali Coast, Kaua'i, 1993.

p. 144 Kilohana Crater, Kaua'i, 1993.

p. 147 Kona Coast, Hawai'i Island, 1993.

p. 152 Waimea Canyon, Kaua'i, 1993.

p. 158 Na Pali Coast, Kaua'i, 1993.

p. 164 Southwest Coast of Moloka'i, 1993.

P. 166 Humpback whale in waters of Hawai'i, by idreamphoto, Shutterstock.

p. 171 Hāna Church, by Massimo Bocchi, Shutterstock.

p. 172 Hāna Bay, by Tuks Medeiros.

p. 182 Double Rainbow at Wai'anapanapa, Maui, by Arnie Kotler.

ACKNOWLEDGMENTS

For the fabled Barbara and Galen Rowell, my parents, Shenna and Julian Meeker, my maternal grandparents, Mary Pearl and Ed S. Hill, and great-grandmother Bowling, each of whom always kept a book nearby; Nancy and Jake Hamon, my first private publishers; for the Kristoffersons, Janie Beggs, the Ed Ruschas, who encouraged me each step of the way; for my fifth-grade teacher and great stimulus, Mrs. Shepard, and my mutual fan, Carolyn Kemble; for John Connolly, the first light in the wilderness of high school and a great role model for a reader.

At Dartmouth, I heard the great and venerable Robert Frost read his poems several times. The new voice of poetry Allen Ginsberg, barely known at the time, read his soon-to-be-famous poem "Howl" and other works to a dozen of us in our professor's living room—a real game changer. It was published that year, in 1956.

I would like to honor all the citizens of Hāna, Maui;
and Fr. Leo Lucero, the Blakes, the Millers,
Jane, Carol, and Annie Owen, the Kelly family, Kathleen
Alioto and her wonderful kids, the Atwood–DeBolt family,
Anne Benoit, Shirine Gill, Louisa Pu,
Calvin Park and family,
Jeannie Pechin, Mimi and Danielle,
Mike and Carolyn Atwood, Patricia Cabellon,
Bob Getzen, Kahikāhealani Wight, the Stockholms,
the Newsoms, the Gettys, the Basses, Kristin Pace, Vernon
White, and all the others I love (you know who you are),
I send you all Aloha, indeed.

I especially want to honor those who made this book happen,
Arnie Kotler, Thea Chalmers, Domenica Alioto,
Lisa Carta, Dorothy and Bob DeBolt,
and not least, Gini Araiza.